THE BODY Christ

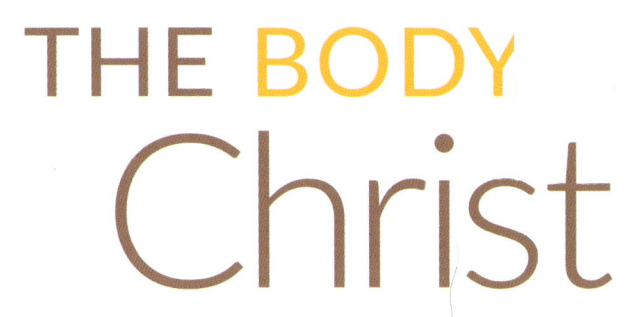

written by
A. W. Mausolf & Monica Ashour

illustrated by
Brian Dumm

Level 6
BOOK 2
Second Edition

TOBET THEOLOGY OF THE BODY EVANGELIZATION TEAM

Dedicated to the Church, including our family and friends, and especially to Mother Mary and Saint John Paul.
Tremendous thanks to all TOBET members over the years. Special thanks to Kathy, Lisa, Sarah, Sr. Mary Angela, CK, and Véronique. We are grateful for consultation work by the translator of the *Theology of the Body*, Dr. Michael Waldstein, as well as Dr. Susan Waldstein. We are also grateful for the consultation work of Katrina J. Zeno, MTS. **With grateful recognition to Sheryl Collmer whose work and insights inspired much of this text.**

For the Ricos

Nihil Obstat: Tomas Fuerte, S.T.L.
Censor Librorum

Imprimatur: +Most Reverend Samuel J. Aquila, S.T.L.
Archbishop of Denver
Denver, Colorado, USA
March 12, 2019

Library of Congress information on file. ISBN 978-1-945845-35-2 • Second Edition

Cover Design: FigDesign • Layout: Emily Gudde • Editor: Dayspring Brock • Associate Editor: Alexis Mausolf

The quote on pg. 17 is from Bishop Robert Barron, "The Mystical Transfiguration of Christ." Feb. 25, 2018, https://www.wordonfire.org/resources/homily/the-mystical-transfiguration-of-christ/4676/. Used with permission.

The quote on pg. 43 is from Pope Benedict XVI. *Deus Caritas est*. Dec. 25, 2005, http://w2.vatican.va/content/benedict-xvi/en/encyclicals/documents/hf_ben-xvi_enc_20051225_deus-caritas-est.html.

Excerpts from the English translation of the *Catechism of the Catholic Church*. New York: Catholic Book Publishing Co., 1994.

Excerpts from the English translation of the *Catechism of the Catholic Church*. New York: Catholic Book Publishing Co., 1994.

Based on John Paul II's *Man and Woman He Created Them: A Theology of the Body*. Trans. Michael Waldstein, Copyright © 2006. Used by permission of Pauline Books & Media, 50 Saint Paul's Ave, Boston, Massachusetts 02130. All rights reserved. www.pauline.org.

All Scripture verses are from the *New American Bible*, Revised Edition (NABRE).

Excerpt from *YOUCAT*, trans. Michael J. Miller. San Francisco: Ignatius Press, 2011. www.ignatius.com. Used with permission.

Printed in the United States of America. © Copyright 2021 Monica Ashour. All rights reserved. No part of this book may be reproduced or transmitted in any form or by any means, electronic or mechanical, including photocopying, recording, or by any information storage and retrieval system without permission in writing from the publisher.

TOBET PRESS

Table of Contents

1 ### Christianity Is for Union — 4
- God's gift of union brings joy.
- Adam and Eve lost union through sin.
- God the Son came to restore union.

2 ### The Incarnate Body of Christ — 14
- God the Son humbled Himself and became human.
- The Incarnation is for union.
- God the Son took on human nature in order to give us a share in His divine nature.

3 ### The Eucharistic Body of Christ — 24
- God the Son humbled Himself and became the Bread of Life.
- The Eucharist is for union.
- God transcends time and space so He can give us His Eucharistic Body in the Mass.

4 ### The Mystical Body of Christ — 38
- God the Son humbles Himself through the members of His Mystical Body.
- The Mystical Body of Christ, the Church, is for union.
- All baptized people are members of the Mystical Body of Christ, the Church.

1 Christianity Is for Union

Belonging

When you come back to school after summer vacation, isn't it great to see your friends again? When you go to practice, doesn't it feel good to be part of the team? When your family gathers for the holidays, doesn't that feeling of belonging make you happy?

That great feeling comes from being in **union** with others. You can be in union with your family, your neighbors, your school, and your fellow citizens. You can be in union with your teams, your classmates, and with your own group of friends. Union brings joy!

God's Inner Life of Love

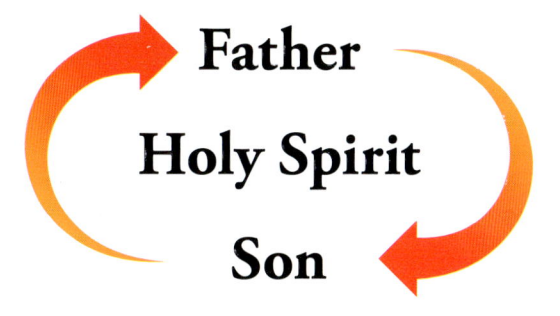

Father ↻ Holy Spirit ↻ Son

The Father **gives** to the Son.

The Son **receives** the Father's Gift of Self and **returns** His own Gift of Self.

The Holy Spirit is the Uncreated **Fruit** of Their Love.

God designed humans to be together, and He wants us to experience the feeling of belonging. St. John Paul says that we most closely resemble God when we are in union with others. Why?

All true union is based on God—three Persons who belong together: Father, Son, and Holy Spirit. No wonder God is love!

The Holy Spirit has guided the Church to the **first** great truth of our Faith—that the Blessed Trinity is three Persons in one union of love. This is not an easy truth to understand. The Trinity is a mystery of the Faith. Welcome to the mystery!

The Gift of Union

God wanted to share the joy of union. So, He created the first humans, Adam and Eve, and gave them an abundance of union. They were in union with God, with each other, within themselves, and with nature.

Union was a gift. Adam and Eve knew that God was a loving Father, the greatest Gift-Giver. They saw every part of creation as a gift, and they knew that they were gifts to each other too.

Fourfold Union
Adam and Eve in the Garden

In Union	Description
with **God**	"God blessed them... and found... everything he had made... very good" (Gen. 1:31).
with **each other**	They were designed for each other.
within **himself** or **herself**	Each person knew perfect harmony in body and spirit.
with **nature**	They lived in the beautiful Garden of Eden with joy and without fear or suffering.

© Copyright 2018 by Monica Ashour. All rights reserved.

"This is *the body: a witness* to creation as a fundamental gift, and therefore a witness *to Love*...."   *Theology of the Body 14:4*

Doubting the Gift

Then Satan came in the form of a serpent to disrupt God's gift of union. He persuaded Adam and Eve to believe his lies. They stopped trusting that God was a loving Father and Gift-Giver. Adam and Eve disobeyed God by eating from the Tree of the Knowledge of Good and Evil.

The first parents of humanity brought darkness and disunion into creation. This is called Original Sin, or The Fall. St. John Paul says that they "doubted the gift." They doubted the gifts of God and of each other. Because of their sin, the union of the world was shattered.

Fourfold Disunion
Adam and Eve after The Fall

Disunion	Description
from **God**	They no longer believed God was a Gift-Giver but thought He was a tyrant. They disobeyed.
from **each other**	They sinned and then blamed each other.
within **himself** or **herself**	Their spirits and bodies worked against each other, resulting in shame; therefore, they hid from God.
from **nature**	They were expelled from the Garden of Eden, and life became hard and dangerous.

© Copyright 2018 by Monica Ashour. All rights reserved.

"...[T]he breaking of the covenant with God in the human heart... [brought disunion]." *Theology of the Body 26:2*

Good Rules Are for Love

Adam and Eve no longer saw that God's commands are for love. They rebelled against their limits, and they rebelled against God.

Yet, God's commands serve as a warning about things that will hurt us. God does not want us to suffer from division, fear, sin, and loss of union. On the contrary, He always wills our good and our happiness.

Because of this, God provides good rules to protect and to guide us. He is like a dad who gives his son a chemistry set—along with a safety lesson. He wants his son to have fun and experiment freely but without accidently blowing up the garage!

What do you think? Do you see God the Father as a good Gift-Giver?

Sin and the Heart

A major consequence of The Fall is that we tend toward sin. When we sin, we break God's rules. Sin is not just about breaking rules, though. Sin breaks union with God; it breaks the Father's heart.

Sin also disrupts the union between people. For example, if one person gossips about another, it breaks the trust between the two of them. Sin breaks a friend's heart.

Moreover, when we sin, it is as if we divide our body from our soul. We know what is right, but instead of doing the right thing, we sin, dividing ourselves. Sin also breaks your own heart.

God's Plan to Save

God made a plan to save us from sin and disunion. He entered into a covenant with the Jewish people and sent them laws and prophets to teach them His commands.

In many prophecies, God promised to send a Savior to bring us back into full union with Him. God's people waited thousands of years for this Savior.

"God therefore chose the Israelite race to be his own people and established a covenant with [them]."
CCC 781

"The redemption of the body… is an object of hope. This hope has been implanted in the human heart… immediately after the first sin."
Theology of the Body 86:2

Who was this promised Savior? In the fullness of time, God Himself entered the world and dwelt among us. The Father sent His own Son to be born a child. He was named Jesus, and He was given the mission to restore the union we had lost through sin: union with God, with each other, within ourselves, and with nature. "How does He do this?" you might ask. The answer: Through His Body!

We can recognize Jesus' Body in three ways:

- His Incarnate Body
- His Eucharistic Body
- His Mystical Body

The Body of Christ matters!

Mission: Write down one good rule from home and one good rule from school. Describe how they limit your freedom. Now write down how they protect you from danger and/or sin. Do they ultimately give you more freedom? Lastly, write down what would happen without these rules. Would there be peace or chaos?

2 The Incarnate Body of Christ

The First Christmas

You have probably heard the story of the Nativity many times. The hosts of angelic choirs, the brilliant star leading Magi from the East, the bewildered shepherds—what was all the excitement about? Who was this Jesus they came to adore?

From all eternity, the Father, Son, and Holy Spirit are Divine Persons in one union. Then, in a startling turn of events, God the Son became human—with a body! His body was brought forth from Mary's body. This is called the Incarnation.

"The fact that *theology also includes the body* should not astonish or surprise anyone who is conscious of the mystery and reality of the Incarnation." *Theology of the Body 23:4*

God's Gift to Us
The Incarnation

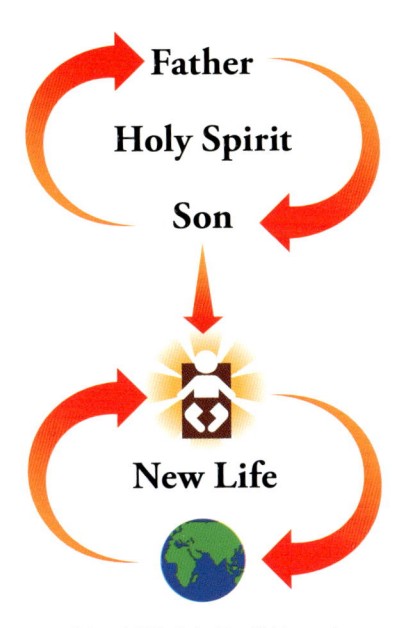

Father
Holy Spirit
Son

New Life

Humbling Himself

The Son humbled Himself and became human. Like all of us, He had a human family. The Holy Family—Jesus, Mary, and Joseph—lived together in union.

Through His body, Jesus felt all the things we feel. He felt hungry and full, sleepy and rested, sad and joyful. For "the Word became flesh and made his dwelling among us" (Jn. 1:14). Jesus, our Savior, came to bring us new life. Yet, He Who was God looked like you and me.

The Incarnation is for union.

The Mystery of the Incarnation

Imagine a classmate of yours saying that he is God. No one would believe him! So, consider how hard it must have been for those who heard that Jesus was God. Those around Him could not grasp how the Eternal God could have a human body.

This led to many misunderstandings. Many people walked away from Jesus because of their false understanding of the Incarnate Body of Christ.

> "The Jews answered him, 'We are not stoning you for a good work but for blasphemy. You, a man, are making yourself God.'" *Jn. 10:33*

- Some people thought Jesus was God, and only **appeared** to be human. **That was false.**
- Some people thought Jesus was like an angel—**not** God and **not** human. **That was false.**
- Some people thought Jesus was born only human, but then **later** became God. **That was false.**

All of these misunderstandings are based on the belief that the body is bad or unworthy of God. But this is not true. Jesus shows us that it is good to be human and that it is good to have a body. He has a human body, like us—for all eternity!

The Holy Spirit has guided the Church to the **second** greatest truth of our Faith—that Jesus Christ is true God and true Man. This is not an easy truth to understand. The Incarnate Body of Christ is a mystery of our Faith. Welcome to the mystery!

"If Jesus were only divine, He could not touch us.
If Jesus were only human, He could not save us."
—Bishop Robert Barron

A False Understanding

Modern culture makes many errors about the body. How does a false understanding of the body still affect us today?

Error: The body is like a canvas or a billboard, so why not decorate or deface ourselves as we choose?

Truth: The body is a gift from God that deserves reverence since we are made in His image and likeness.

Error: The body is like a machine, so why not "plug in" to devices and forget about everyone else?

Truth: The body is made for union. We are designed to interact with others and not to isolate ourselves.

Do you see how much the body matters?

"God took on a human body in Jesus; this was not mere appearance... he became truly human. Nor are there two different persons in Christ, one human and one Divine. Contrary to heresy, the Church believes that Jesus is at the same time true God and true man in one person, without division or confusion."
YOUCAT 77

19

The Reason Behind the Incarnation

Why would the All-Powerful, All-Knowing, All-Present Son of God humble Himself to become human? To have union with us! It is a fact that only those of the same nature can be in union. For example, a fox can only find full union with other foxes or a chicken with other chickens. Why? They share the same nature. Can there be close union between cats and rats? What about bees and bears? Between foxes and fowl? No—they are not of the same nature. Such close union is only possible between those of the same nature.

A New Nature

Since The Fall of Adam and Eve, humans no longer share God's nature, so they are no longer in union with God. We are born with Original Sin, which separates us from Him. But God does not give up on us.

In a supreme act of love through the Gift of Self, God the Son took on human nature in order to give us a share in His divine nature. While remaining divine, He became human—with a human body!

Because of Jesus, we can now be in union with God. Through Baptism, we receive new life as the sons and daughters of God, and so we have union with Him again.

There is Union!

The Son's Incarnate Body shows that not only do human bodies matter, but human actions also matter. When we follow His commands with our bodily actions, we gain closer union with others. What does this look like?

Jesus says, "Do to others whatever you would have them do to you" (Mt. 7:12). When you sacrifice some of your time at recess to help a classmate with his math homework… just like that, there is union!

Jesus says, "The first will be last and the last will be first" (see Mt. 20:16). When you give the gift of self and let your little sister have the first ice cream cone… just like that, there is union!

"In Baptism, we become members of the Body of Christ, sisters and brothers of our Redeemer, and children of God."
YOUCAT 200

This Is My Body: The Incarnation

🔔 The Incarnation Is for Heaven

The Son of God became human so that humans can become sons and daughters of God. When we say that Jesus "opened the gates of Heaven," that means that all people of all times who choose to say "yes" to Jesus' Gift can share in eternal life with God. The Incarnate Body of Christ leads us to Heaven.

Based on Adrienne von Speyr's Most Important Words in the Universe. © Copyright 2021 by Monica Ashour. All rights reserved.

Mission: Since Jesus was born with a body like us, what do you think He experienced? Laughter? Hunger? Sadness? Fear? What feelings might you have in common with Him? Spend some time thinking about Jesus at your age. What was His life like? How was His life similar to yours? Share with Jesus what you are experiencing. He knows, and He cares.

3 The Eucharistic Body of Christ

Are We Too Late?

The Son of God lived on Earth, died on the cross, and rose from the dead over 2,000 years ago. That means we can no longer meet Jesus face-to-face in the same way His disciples did. Are we 2,000 years too late? Not at all. As always, God finds a way to reach us. From Heaven to Earth and now to the Eucharist!

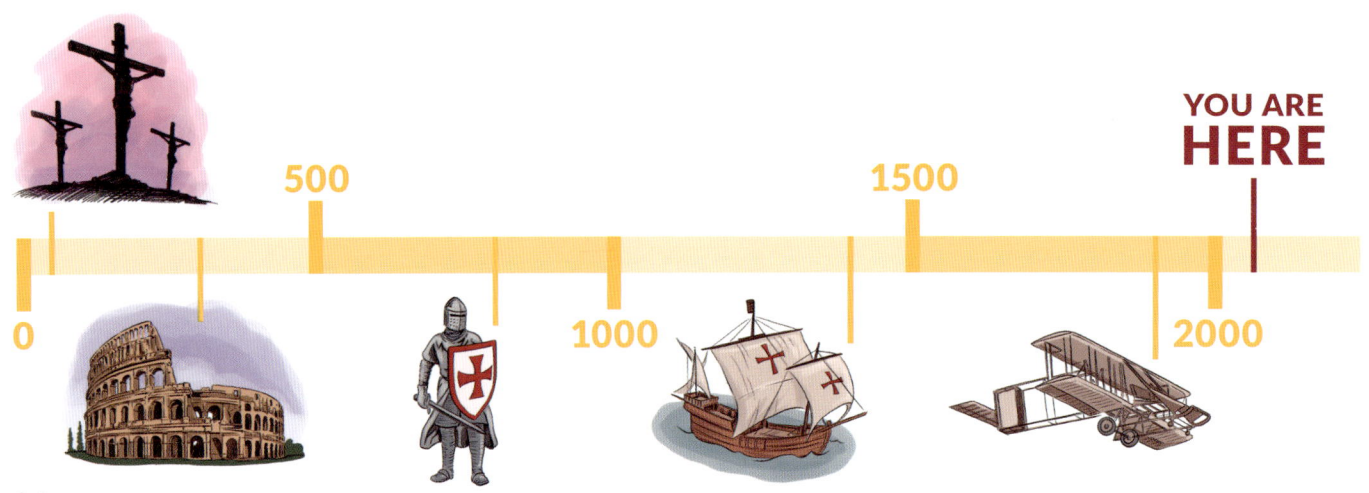

YOU ARE HERE

0 — 500 — 1000 — 1500 — 2000

"The redemption of the body has already been completed in Christ, not just after death but present [now to all.]"

Theology of the Body 86:3

God's Gift to Us
The Eucharist

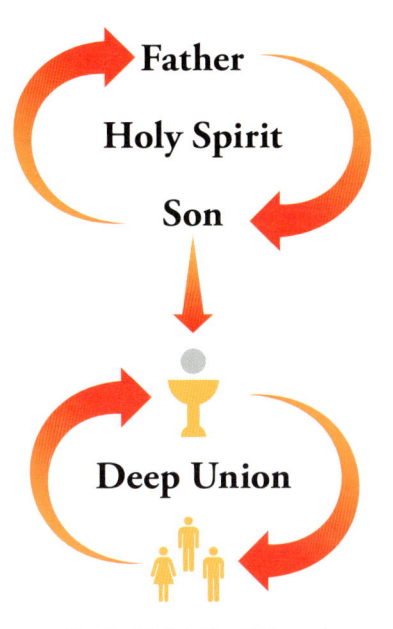

Father
Holy Spirit
Son

Deep Union

Humbling Himself

Not only did the Son become human as a baby for us, but the Son even humbled Himself to become the Bread of Life.

Jesus says, "I am the Bread of Life. He who eats my flesh and drinks my blood will never die" (see Jn. 6:35–59). The Eternal God reaches us in the humble appearance of bread, so that deeper union with Him becomes possible.

The Eucharist is for union.

© Copyright 2018 by Monica Ashour. All rights reserved.

Bread of Life

The Eucharist, instituted at the Last Supper, is at the heart of our Faith and has always been part of God's plan. There are clues in Scripture! Look how many times in the Bible we can find "bread" coming from Heaven.

In the Old Testament, God sent manna to feed His people in the desert. This bread that came from the sky was a foreshadowing of Jesus' future Gift of Himself in the Eucharist since He is the "Bread from Heaven."

When Jesus was born, He was laid in a manger in Bethlehem, a town whose name means "House of Bread." The manger itself was designed to hold food. At Jesus' birth, it held Him, Who is Food for our eternal life.

The miracle of Jesus' multiplication of loaves foreshadows the fact that Jesus, the Bread of Life, is distributed to millions of people in the Eucharist. He is shared with the entire world every day.

> "Christ nourishes the Church with his Body precisely in the Eucharist."
> *Theology of the Body 99:1*

27

The Mystery of the Eucharist

Imagine a classmate of yours saying that he is the bread that came down from Heaven. No one would believe him! How strange it must have been for those who heard Jesus say, "I am the bread of life... and the bread that I give is my flesh for the life of the world" (Jn. 6:48–51). The people listening to Jesus were shocked! They murmured, saying, "How can this man give us his flesh to eat?" They could not understand why He would give His Body and Blood for us. This has led to many misunderstandings. Many people have walked away from Jesus because of their false understanding of the Eucharistic Body of Christ.

- Some people think God is present **only spiritually** in the Eucharist. **That is false**.
- Some people think the Eucharist is just **bread**, a mere symbol or reminder of Jesus. **That is false**.
- Some people think the Eucharist is a **combination** of Jesus' Body and of bread. **That is false**.
- Some people think that **their faith** is what turns the bread into the Body of Christ. **That is false**.

The Holy Spirit has guided the Church to the **third** greatest truth of our Faith—that Jesus Christ, true God and true Man—is bodily present in the Eucharist. The Eucharist **is** the real Body and Blood of Jesus Christ and only appears to be bread and wine.

This is not an easy truth to understand. The Eucharistic Body of Christ is a mystery of our Faith. Welcome to the mystery!

🍷 A False Understanding

How does a false understanding of the Eucharist still affect us today?

Error: The Eucharist is only bread, so why show reverence? Why not chew gum, text, talk to friends, and daydream at Mass if the Eucharist is just bread?

Truth: Since the Eucharist **is** the Body of Christ, **reverence** is the right response. At Mass we genuflect, pray, respond in the liturgy, and listen attentively to God speaking to us.

Error: The Eucharist is not Jesus Christ, so why bother going to Mass?

Truth: Since the Eucharist **is** Jesus Christ—Body, Blood, Soul, and Divinity—His bodily presence deserves the response of our bodily presence. Ultimately, we know that we have a Body-to-body encounter with Our Lord in the Eucharist.

🏆 The Reason Behind the Eucharist

Why would the All-Powerful, All-Knowing, All-Present Son of God humble Himself to become the Bread of Life?—To have union with us! Have you ever dreamed of traveling in a time machine? The Mass is like a time-machine. When you kneel in prayer during the Consecration, imagine that this is the moment when the time machine activates. Imagine the kneeler flying you 2,000 years back in time to Calvary. You see Jesus crucified before you.

You see Mother Mary, St. John, and Mary Magdalene at the foot of the cross. Christ's Body speaks a language, saying to each of us: *This is My Body, given up as a Gift for you.* Jesus also says this at Mass when the priest speaks for Him: *This is My Body, given up for you.* God transcends time and space so that He can actually give us His Eucharistic Body. He gives Himself as a gift to you at every Mass!

31

The Gift of Self at Mass

Eucharist means "thanksgiving." We give thanks for Jesus' Gift of Himself to us. But He is not the only one who gives. You are a gift to Him as well! At Mass, the bread and wine are presented to the priest for consecration. At this point, you can offer Jesus yourself, your family, your friends, your schoolwork, your worries, and your joys. Jesus receives it all. Then Jesus offers Himself, including you and all you offer, as a Gift to the Father.

The Father receives everything from His Son. In return, the Father gives His own Gift of Self through the Holy Spirit. Just as the bread and wine are transformed into the Eucharist, you and all you gave to Jesus are now transformed by grace.

The next time you are at Mass, unite yourself with Christ on the altar. Be assured that, even if it doesn't feel like something has happened, a transformation has really occurred.

"The Eucharist is 'the source and summit of the Christian life.'" *CCC 1324*

The Mass in Our Lives

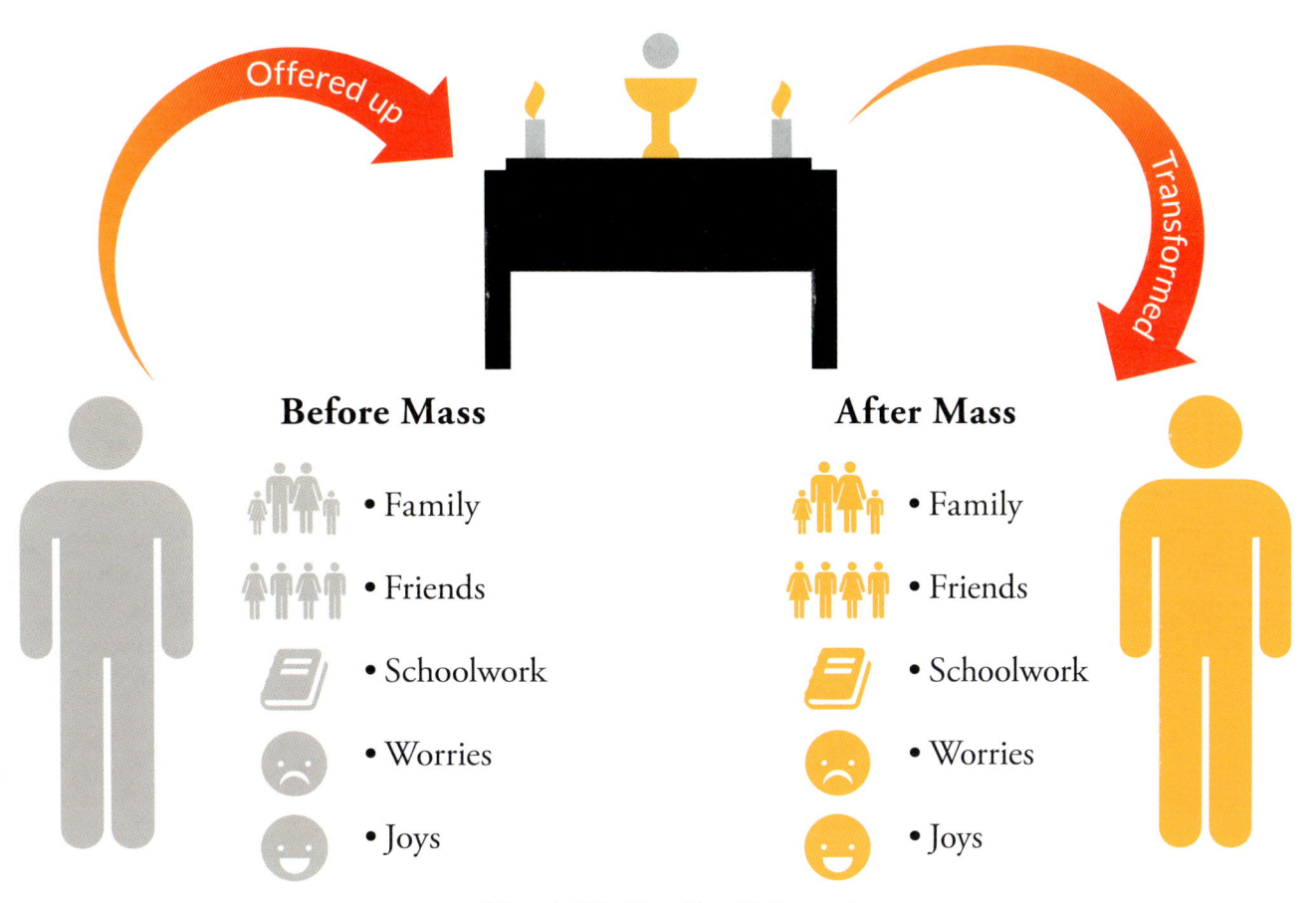

Before Mass
- Family
- Friends
- Schoolwork
- Worries
- Joys

Offered up

Transformed

After Mass
- Family
- Friends
- Schoolwork
- Worries
- Joys

© Copyright 2019 by Monica Ashour. All rights reserved.

Prayer and the Mass

Did you know that every single prayer, big or small, is directed toward Jesus? Whether you pray alone or with others, He is listening.

When you read Scripture or pray the rosary or just talk to God in your heart, your prayers reach Jesus, Who presents them to the Father at Holy Mass.

Sacramental Vision of the Eucharist

🍷 Why the Eucharist?

Jesus' Eucharistic Body fills us with grace, restores virtue, and separates us from sin.

Holy Communion unites us more strongly with God. It is through our union with Jesus Christ that we also have deeper union with others.

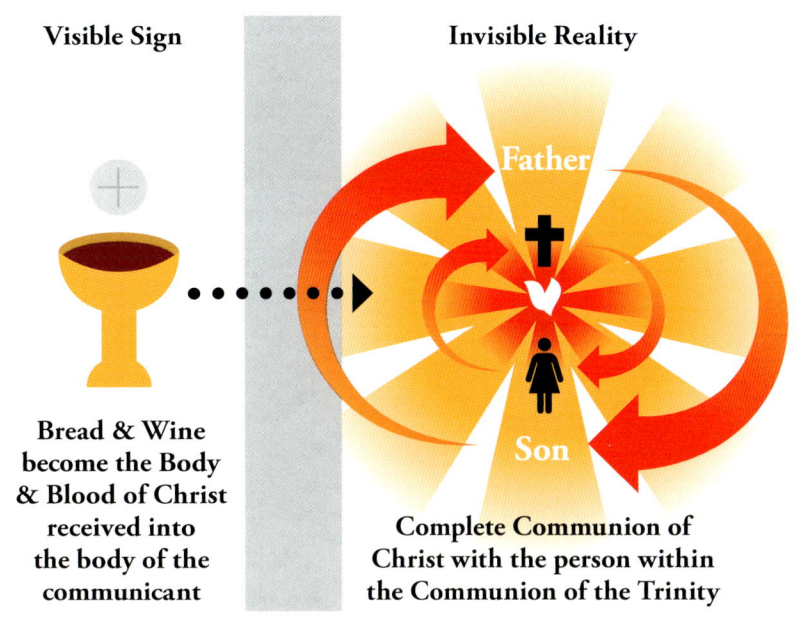

Visible Sign | **Invisible Reality**

Bread & Wine become the Body & Blood of Christ received into the body of the communicant

Complete Communion of Christ with the person within the Communion of the Trinity

Based on *TOB* 87:5; 93:3-7; 98:1-3. © Copyright 2014 by Monica Ashour. All rights reserved.

> "Holy Eucharist is the sacrament in which Jesus gives us his Body and Blood, so that we too might give ourselves to him in love and be united with him.... In this way we are joined with the one Body of Christ, the Church." — *YOUCAT 208*

There is Union!

Jesus shows us that our bodies are good. In fact, God finds the human body so good that He is willing to enter into our bodies through the Eucharist. God's Gift of the Body of Christ is for union.

Jesus says, "He who eats my flesh abides in me and I in him" (Jn. 6:56). When you receive the Eucharist, you stay with Him and He stays with you… just like that, there is union!

Jesus says, "I am the vine, you are the branches" (Jn. 15:5). When you receive the Eucharist, you are united with all Christians throughout the world… just like that, there is union!

Mass: The Greatest Union

© Copyright 2019 by Monica Ashour. All rights reserved.

Jesus says, "Whoever eats my flesh and drinks my blood has eternal life, and I will raise him on the last day" (Jn. 6:54). When you receive the Eucharist, you prepare for Heaven, where you will meet Jesus, Mary, the angels, and all the saints… just like that, there is eternal union!

This Is My Body: The Eucharist

🍷 The Eucharist Is for Heaven

The Son of God becomes the Bread of Life for us so that we can enjoy eternal life with Him. Jesus is our *viaticum*, our "Bread for the Journey."

Heaven is all about union. Jesus prepares us for eternal union with Him in His Gift of the Eucharist. The Eucharistic Body of Christ leads us to Heaven.

Based on Adrienne von Speyr's Most Important Words in the Universe. © Copyright 2013 by Monica Ashour. All rights reserved.

Mission: Make it your mission to be aware of the two parts of the Mass: the Liturgy of the Word and the Liturgy of the Eucharist. Prepare to hear Christ proclaimed in the first part when you receive Him in the Word. Grow even closer to Christ in the second part when you receive Him in the Eucharist.

4 The Mystical Body of Christ

An Ocean of Love

Jesus wants to make sure that all people can find a way to Him, despite the limits of space and time. He has provided yet another way for His Body to be present in the world—through you and me!

Have you ever stood at the edge of an ocean, in awe of its immensity? Just as a body of water, like an ocean, is made of many, many individual droplets, Christ's Mystical Body, the Church, is made up of many, many individuals. Each of us is a member of the Body of Christ. The word *mystical* is related to the word *mystery*.

We call the Church the Mystical Body of Christ because of the mysterious union between Christ and His people. He is the head, and we are the members of His Body.

"...[T]he eternal mystery has passed from the state of 'hiddenness in God' to the phase of revelation.... Christ... reveals the eternal mystery and accomplishes it among men and women."   *Theology of the Body 94:3*

God's Gift to Us
The Mystical Body

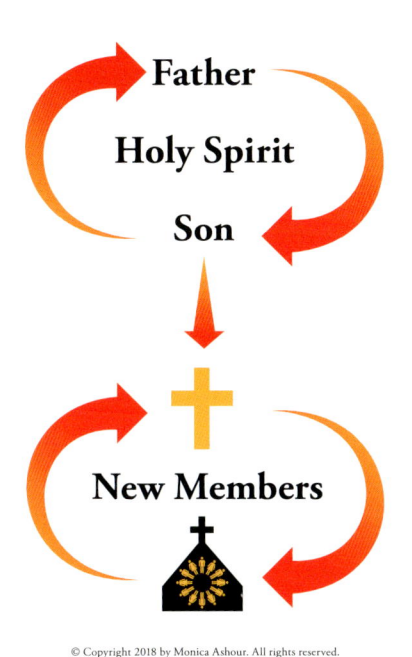

Father
Holy Spirit
Son

New Members

Humbling Himself

Not only did the Son become human as a baby for us, and not only did the Son become the Bread of Life for us, but, still today, He humbles Himself to be present through the members of His Mystical Body.

The Eternal God reaches the world through ordinary people in His Church. Through Baptism, new members extend Christ's love to others.

The Mystical Body of Christ, the Church, is for union.

Christ and His Body

☀ The Mystery of the Mystical Body

Imagine a classmate of yours saying that what you do to others, you do to him. No one would believe him! How hard it must have been for those who heard that Jesus was one Body with His Church! They could not understand how someone with a body could be one with everyone else.

This has led to many misunderstandings. Many have walked away from Jesus because of their false understanding of the Church as the Mystical Body of Christ.

© Copyright 2021 by Monica Ashour. All rights reserved.

> "Now you are Christ's body, and individually parts of it." 1 Cor. 12:27

- Some people think the Church has **only** a spiritual connection to God, and there is no physical connection present. **That is false**.
- Some people think the Church is **not necessary**. They think it is enough to be alone with God, and they do not need union with others in common worship. **That is false**.
- Some people think that the Church is **only** man-made and **not** guided by God. **That is false**.

The Holy Spirit has guided the Church to the **fourth** greatest truth of our Faith—that Jesus Christ is one with His Mystical Body, the Church.

We are one with Jesus' Body. This is not an easy truth to understand. The Body of Christ, the Church, is a mystery of our Faith. Welcome to the mystery!

> "...[T]he church of the living God [is] the pillar and foundation of truth."
> 1 Tim. 3:15

✳ A False Understanding

How does a false understanding of the Mystical Body of Christ still affect us today?

Error: The Church is only spiritual, so why do we need the sacraments that we can see, touch, hear, smell, and taste with our bodies?

Truth: The Church and the sacraments **are both physical and spiritual** because we are both body and spirit.

Error: The Church is only man-made, so why obey her teachings?

Truth: The Church **is founded by Jesus and led by the Holy Spirit**. Since the Church **is** the Body of Christ, obedience to Her teachings and Tradition frees us to love and to live in union with God and others.

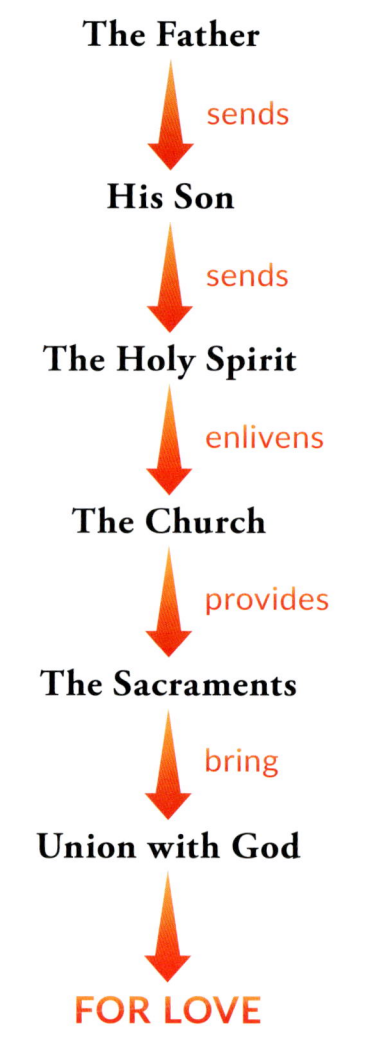

The Father
↓ sends
His Son
↓ sends
The Holy Spirit
↓ enlivens
The Church
↓ provides
The Sacraments
↓ bring
Union with God
↓
FOR LOVE

© Copyright 2019 by Monica Ashour. All rights reserved.

"...[T]he 'Word' again becomes 'flesh'... in a real sense whenever human beings act out of authentic love...."
—Joseph Ratzinger
(Pope Benedict XVI)

✺ The Reason Behind The Mystical Body

Why would the All-Powerful, All-Knowing, All-Present Son of God humble Himself by allowing us small and sinful creatures to be His Body?—To have union with us! We **are** His Mystical Body.

In the early days of the Church, a man named Saul persecuted many Christians. He did not understand they were members of the Body of Christ.

On the road to Damascus, where he was planning to arrest a number of Christians and "bring them back in chains," he was blinded by a sudden light and fell down.

Jesus spoke to him: "Saul, Saul, why are you persecuting me?" "Who are you, Sir?" said Saul. "I am Jesus, whom you are persecuting" (see Acts 9:1–5).

> "Because in Christ we are one Body, we live in a communion that encompasses heaven and earth." — *YOUCAT 146*

Did you notice that Jesus said, "Why are you persecuting **me**?" Wasn't Saul persecuting the Christians? Jesus meant that all Christians have union with Him in His Mystical Body.

Jesus told Saul to be baptized. After Baptism, Saul met with the apostles, including St. Peter, the first pope—the visible head of the Mystical Body. Saul was later called Paul and became a great saint, writing much of the New Testament and bringing many people into the Church.

All baptized people are members of the Mystical Body of Christ—the Church.

One Body in Christ

A popular quote of St. Teresa of Avila is "Christ has no body now on earth but yours. No hands, no feet but yours."

Think about your own body. You have arms, legs, feet, hands, heart, and lungs. They belong and work together, each with its own function. Each helps to keep the body healthy and whole.

Scripture says that we are many parts but one body (see I Cor. 12). As your own body has many parts, so Christ's Mystical Body has many members. Each person has his or her own gifts and mission. We belong and work together. Each of us helps to keep the Body of Christ healthy and whole.

In a well-known story, St. Martin of Tours cut his cloak in half to share with a beggar who was shivering in the cold. That night, he saw Christ in a dream, wearing half of the cloak. St. Martin understood that by giving to the poor man, he had given a gift to Jesus.

☀ There Is Union!

Christ brings about union through His Mystical Body. Jesus says, "I was hungry and you gave me food, I was thirsty and you gave me drink" (Mt. 25:35). When you relieve the sufferings of others, you bring Christ to them… just like that, there is union!

Jesus says, "That which you did to the least of my brethren, you did to me" (see Mt. 25:40). When you are a friend to those left out, you are a friend to Jesus… just like that, there is union!

This is My Body: The Mystical Body

© Copyright 2018 by Monica Ashour. All rights reserved.

"Every Holy Communion unites me more deeply with Christ, makes me a living member of the Body of Christ, renews the graces I received in Baptism and Confirmation, and fortifies me for the battle against sin." YOUCAT 221

The Mystical Body of Christ Is for Heaven

The Son of God allows us to be members of His Body so that we can enjoy eternal life with Him. The Mystical Body of Christ leads us to Heaven. Eternal union is made possible through the Body of Christ!

This Is My Body

© Copyright 2018 by Monica Ashour. All rights reserved.

CATHOLIC TREASURE BOX

The Church Honors Mary

The Church has deepened our understanding of Mary, giving her titles such as "Star of the Sea" or "Refuge of Sinners." Some titles have a direct connection to the Body of Christ.

- Mary is the "Mother of God" and "Ark of the Covenant."

- Mary is "Our Lady of the Blessed Sacrament" and "Our Lady of the Precious Blood."

- Mary is "Mother of the Church" and "Queen of all Saints."